10 TOP TIPS

for **Making Introductions**

Lindsey Dunbar

BAAF
ADOPTION
& FOSTERING

Published by
**British Association for Adoption & Fostering
(BAAF)**
Saffron House
6–10 Kirby Street
London EC1N 8TS
www.baaf.org.uk

Charity registration 275689 (England and Wales)
and SC039337 (Scotland)

British Library Cataloguing in Publication Data
A catalogue record for this book is available from the British Library

ISBN 978 1 905664 66 5

Project management by Jo Francis, BAAF
Designed by Andrew Haig & Associates
Typeset by Fravashi Aga
Printed in Great Britain by T J International Ltd
Trade distribution by Turnaround Publisher Services, Unit 3,
Olympia Trading Estate, Coburg Road, London N22 6TZ

BAAF is the leading UK-wide membership organisation for all those
concerned with adoption, fostering and child care issues.

The paper used for the text pages of this book is FSC certified.
FSC (The Forest Stewardship Council) is an international network
to promote responsible management of the world's forests.

Printed on totally chlorine-free paper.

FSC
Mixed Sources
Product group from well-managed
forests and other controlled sources

Cert no. SGS-COC-2482
www.fsc.org
© 1996 Forest Stewardship Council

Contents

This series

Ten Top Tips on Making Introductions is the sixth title in BAAF's *Ten Top Tips* series. This series tackles some fundamental issues in the area of adoption and fostering with the aim of presenting them in a quick reference format. Previous titles are:

- *Ten Top Tips for Placing Children*, by Hedi Argent
- *Ten Top Tips for Managing Contact*, by Henrietta Bond
- *Ten Top Tips for Finding Families*, by Jennifer Cousins
- *Ten Top Tips for Placing Siblings*, by Hedi Argent
- *Ten Top Tips for Preparing Care Leavers*, by Henrietta Bond

Details are available on www.baaf.org.uk.

The next title to be published in the series will be *Ten Top Tips for Managing Kinship Placements,* by Hedi Argent.

Acknowledgements

I would like to thank all the children, families and professionals I
have had the privilege to work with over my years as a social worker.
A particular thanks has to go to all my colleagues in the North West
of England. I am indebted to many people, too many to mention
here.They know who they are! I am grateful to them for all I have
been able to learn over the years and especially to the many families
who were generous enough to share their story with me. Many thanks
also to Julia Brown, Adoption Manager at Slough Borough Council,
and to Marjorie Morrison, of BAAF's Publications Advisory Group,
for their careful reading of the script and valuable suggestions, and
to Hedi Argent for her editorial input. Special thanks to Ciaran, Daniel
and John for their patience during the compilation of this book and
for their assistance with computing. Perhaps you can teach an old dog
new tricks after all!

Any unattributed quotations in this book have been taken from
personal communication.

Note about the author

Lindsey Dunbar is a Trainer/Consultant for BAAF in the North West of
England. Lindsey became a social worker in 1984. Her professional
roles have included residential work with children, child protection,
inspection and, since 1995, specialism in fostering and adoption work.
Lindsey has a particular interest in how we successfully enable children
to move into permanent placements.

An introduction to introductions

Perhaps this is akin to holding your newborn baby in your arms for that very first time. The moment will stay with me forever, of that I'm sure. It is one of those landmarks in our lives that we will re-live a thousand times over.

(Adopter on first meeting her four-year-old son to-be (James, 2006, p 82))

Introductions are a normal part of everyday life. The chances are that we meet and are introduced to people without anything remarkable having happened. We are introduced to people who may become colleagues, acquaintances or friends, or to someone we will never see again. We may even be introduced to a member of our family whom we haven't met before. If we are lucky, we will be introduced to a future partner in life – or we may introduce ourselves if we particularly like the look of them. The only people we are sure not to be introduced to are our parents or our children. That is, not unless we adopt or are adopted. One adopter described being introduced to her son as 'a surreal experience'.

Having to be introduced to your parents or to your child is a special, serious business, and we had better take it very seriously. Good introductions are a lynchpin of successful placements and require the most careful joint planning, sensitive management and support. This book sets out to explore best practice in introductions leading to permanent placements. It does not aim to be either an academic textbook or a comprehensive manual; in ten short sections it examines the purpose of introductions and how we can lay solid foundations for children to become fully integrated members of new families.

Generally, introductions bring together the work of several parties: adopters, foster carers, social workers and other professionals. Each party may hold a view of how introductions are to be managed and what is best for the child. It is only through careful negotiation and understanding of needs that we can devise an agreed and workable plan for each individual child. The aim of this book is to ensure that we keep the child central to the whole process.

Placements, for any child in the looked after system, can trigger a wide variety of feelings. Children may feel excitement at moving to their new "forever" family, but also experience great fear and anxiety at having to move away from a settled foster placement. Or their feelings may have been blunted by too many previous moves, so that they cannot properly engage with the next one. It is most important from the outset that all the adults concerned with introductions understand and anticipate that all transitions will involve a degree of loss for children.

Introductions are a culmination of all the work that must take place between linking a child with a family and confirming a match. Argent and Coleman (2006, p 11) state:

> *No-one can be a parent to any or every child between the age of three and five or to any other category of children. Every child is a singular person*

> *and families need the opportunity to "learn the child" however long it takes after linking and before introductions.*

This book concerns itself primarily with moving children into adoptive or permanent foster placements, but many of the principles involved and outlined here could equally be applied to "family and friends" placements. After all, the ultimate aim is to move children successfully into a stable and enduring situation.

I am indebted to all the families I have had the privilege of working with during my 25 years in social work. They have been the best teachers of what does and doesn't work in the permanent placement of children, and they have taught me about the significance of introductions. Only an adopter can tell us how it feels:

> *It's like nothing else. There she was, standing in the doorway, waving to us. What could she really understand about having a new mummy and daddy? She was so vulnerable, we were so scared. We could still have turned back but there was this little person and we felt totally responsible for her already.*
>
> *(Adoptive parent)*

Lindsey Dunbar

February 2009

TIP 1

One size won't fit all!

It makes sense to begin by thinking about what we are seeking to achieve. The purpose of introductions can be seen to include:

- Giving an opportunity for the prospective family and the child to learn about one another at first hand, and to begin to experience what it might be like to live together.
- Supporting the child to make a gradual transition between current and future carers.
- Encouraging the new family to become familiar with the child's signals and routines.
- Giving an opportunity to child and family to begin to build positive attachment patterns.
- Enabling current carers to feel confident enough to let go and prospective carers to be confident enough to proceed.
- Coming to an agreement with all parties about the timing and details of placement.

The child's needs

We can all appreciate that how a baby of 13 months will need to be moved on will be different from moving a sibling group aged four and six years, or children over seven years old. Clearly there can be no general rules about the way in which introductions should be planned and managed. As each child is unique, so will be each introduction plan. But we can extrapolate some guidelines from our own experience and understanding of child development.

Byrne (2000, p 11–12) tells us:

> *Practice is informed by child development and generally, the younger the child, the shorter and more intensive the introductory process.*
>
> *However, care should be taken not to collude with rushed arrangements: disruption experiences as well as research (Lowe et al, 1999, Thomas et al, 1999) show that both children and adopters often feel that placements have been arranged too hurriedly. There may be good reasons for bringing forward a placement date, such as when both child and family feel ready and there is general agreement that to prolong introductions would serve no useful purpose. Yet other influences and pressures may result in precipitous action being taken that may not be in the interests of child or family.*

Byrne goes on to say (p 13):

> *The impact of violence, abuse, neglect and discontinuity of care cannot be ignored for any child and one of the most dangerous assumptions that social workers can make is to think that, because of*

> *their age, very young children must be less*
> *traumatised. This may be so if the child has*
> *experienced a protective and nurturing relationship*
> *in the midst of deprivation and risk; otherwise the*
> *implications of poor early care need both attention*
> *and remedial action.*

If we consider children's needs at different developmental ages, we can see the following differences.

Children 0–18 months

- Main task – to build feelings of safety, security and trust in other human beings.
- Sensitive caregiver will be attuned to the baby's behaviour, reactions and rhythms.
- Babies of this age cannot understand change – they can only "feel" it.
- Babies may experience loss of usual carers as total abandonment and be extremely distressed.

Implications for introductions

- Create familiar sensory experiences, i.e. how things look, smell and feel.
- Keep the baby in the same routine as in the foster home, even if this doesn't fit in easily with the adopters' lifestyle. There will be plenty of time to make gradual changes later. It can be difficult to hear as a new adoptive parent that the very things you expected to have control over, such as the baby's routine, feeding, bathing and bedtimes will be dictated by what the child has been used to in the previous foster home. However, adopters should understand that "tuning in" to the child's needs will promote strong attachments far more quickly than trying to impose unfamiliar routines.
- Use the same washing powder so that bedding and clothing feel and smell the same.
- Keep the foster carers in the picture as much as possible; an infant

will not understand the reasons for sudden separation.

● Allow the child to grieve while offering comfort.

Schofield and Beek (2006, p 56) suggest:

> *...talking to the infant through difficult moments and putting the infant's feelings into words, alongside being available and caring, may be helpful, for example, 'I know you don't really know me yet and this must all seem very strange to you and I guess you must be missing your mum/brother/ foster carer but I'm going to make you comfortable and you'll feel happier in a while'.*

The purpose of talking in this way is to keep the new carer focused on the infant's feelings and to demonstrate to others in the family circle that the baby's upset is understandable and can be contained with sensitive care. It is important to remember that very young children have few internal "coping" skills, so adults have to cope with difficulties on their behalf.

Oates describes (2007) how this is highlighted in Fonagy's work:

> *A caregiver's reflective functioning ability leads them to show in their behaviour and speech that they are actively thinking about their child's inner world and it has been argued that this can help a child to develop the ability to regulate emotions, an important skill in forming good relationships.*

And one adopter, during introductions to a one-year-old, said:

> *It started every time, as soon as his foster carer left.*

> *It was such deep sobbing; it was heartbreaking. All we could do was hold him and rock him and try to soothe him. It was only after a long time, he'd let me comfort him.*

Children 18 months–3 years

Children in this age range go through remarkable developmental changes. They begin to have a sense of themselves as separate from others, develop language skills and become increasingly mobile. They are capable of showing a greater variety of emotions, including anger, fear, sadness and frustration.

According to Schofield and Beek (2006, p 57):

> *One of the challenges for this age period for caregivers and children is that the toddler can sense an exciting ability to be more active and autonomous, to do so much more, and yet needs help to be kept safe and contained. They can toddle towards the fire or the gate but need to be prevented from endangering themselves, with "no" becoming an increasing part of parental vocabulary.*

Many children who come into care at this stage show impaired development due to abuse or neglect and may have limited speech, poor growth due to a lack of food or the wrong type of food, very poor interacting skills and lack any idea of how to play.

It is important to remember that a young child who has been abused or neglected has no means of making sense of the adult's behaviour towards them, and the strategies they have adopted to cope with this treatment may persist even when placed in a caring household. For instance, if you have learned that crying makes your parent angry, then you are likely to learn not to show emotion; similarly, if you have learned that by persistent whingeing you can grind an adult down into giving you whatever it is you want, then you are likely to go on whingeing.

Even if children of this age make huge strides when they come into foster care, they may regress to earlier behaviours when they have to move again. Children who have been toilet-trained may begin to have numerous "accidents", may over- or under-eat, have poor sleep patterns or find everything a source of upset. Naturally this can be very distressing for new parents, who probably fear they are doing something wrong or somehow failing the child.

As with much younger children, it is therefore imperative that established routines are retained and confirmed by the new family during introductions. Familiar objects, bedding from the foster home, photographs of significant people in the child's life, favourite toys and clothes can all help to ease the transition.

> *Four-year-old Danya didn't seem to pay much attention to anything during introductions. But years later, when his adoptive father came across an old pair of shoes at the back of a cupboard, Danya said: 'You wore those shoes every time you came to visit me in my foster home'.*

Schofield and Beek (2006, p 63) advise that during introductions:

> *...the overall parenting task is to provide a very intensively nurturing environment, to build a relationship of trust and gradually build in support for exploration and fun, enabling the child to achieve a gradual return to previous levels of competence.*

Children 3–5 years

Children of this age, who have secure attachments, are likely to be confident within small group settings such as the family unit or a small nursery school. Nevertheless, the absence of a familiar adult can make a child feel anxious and vulnerable. New situations tend to be very threatening, and distressing memories of previous moves, for example, removal from birth parents may be triggered by another change. However, children at this stage will, generally, have more language and will often show great interest in a book or DVD made by the new family, if this is used by the foster carer prior to introductions.

One prospective adopter made a family book of photographs showing themselves in each of the rooms of the "new" house. On each page "Eddie the Teddy" was hidden somewhere in the picture. On the first day of introductions, the adopters took Eddie the Teddy with them to meet their new child and they wore the same clothes they had worn in the photographs. By reading and re-reading the book to the child, the foster carer ensured that Eddie the Teddy became a firm favourite, as did the adopters!

Children of this age don't have a sophisticated concept of time, but drawing a simple calendar outlining what the child will be doing each day during introductions can help. Children can sometimes relate to how many "sleeps" it is before something happens.

Again, the role of the foster carer will be central. They can assist the new parent(s) to learn all about the child's routines, likes, dislikes and fears, and they can reassure the child about the move to their new home.

Children 5–10 years

Children of this age can begin to build a sense of themselves in different settings – at school, with friends, in a football club or as Cubs or Brownies.

But children who have a poor early start in life often find such settings difficult. They may not understand the "rules"; they may overwhelm other children in their eagerness to make friends or, alternatively, show signs of not knowing how to make friends or interact at all. At the upper end of this age range, they may have a sense that being in foster care makes them different from other children. They may have some understanding of why they couldn't continue to live with their birth parents and have a sense of right and wrong. They may worry that it is "wrong" not to live with their birth family and that, perhaps, it is their own fault. Depending on the messages they have been given by adults, some children can be made to feel guilty or ashamed that they are in the care system.

Romaine *et al* (2007, p 97) write:

> *The most important message that a child needs to have from all parties is permission to form attachments to new parents. Older children may feel particularly anxious about this if they are afraid of hurting their present carers or birth family members. Foster carers must be given the opportunity to talk through their feelings about letting the child go.*

It is vital that the foster carer's supervising social worker ensures that the carer has the opportunity to say how they feel about the impending move. Most foster carers talk of this as a bittersweet time. They may be delighted for the child that a permanent family has been identified, but at the same time upset at the prospect of losing a child that they and their family have grown extremely fond of. Clearly, this is likely to be particularly the case when a child has been in placement for a long time or where a child has formed extremely close bonds with family members. We have to ensure that we acknowledge the vital role the foster carer has had in the child's life and allow the carer to express ambivalent feelings, which will, in turn, enable the child to feel sad as well as glad.

Romaine *et al* (2007, p 97) observe, when thinking about older children:

> *There can be a tendency to talk to children about all the good things that moving to a permanent family will bring and avoid any painful ambivalent feelings a child might have. It will be more helpful if children are allowed to express and discuss negative feelings as well as positive ones, to avoid them receiving a message that negative feelings are not valid or acceptable. If foster carers say that they will miss the child and be sad when they go but also be glad that they will have a family of their own, it will give the child permission to have similar feelings and to express them.*

Good practice points

- Consider what developmental stage the child is at.
- Consider their history of moves – how many, what were the circumstances, how traumatic was it for the child?
- What do previous moves tell us when thinking about how to introduce the child to their permanent placement?
- Prepare the adopters/permanent carers for the fact that the child is likely to be experiencing huge feelings of loss at the time of the transition.
- Ensure that a detailed outline of the child's routine is available, in writing, for the new family. Include likes, dislikes, favourite TV programmes, words for particular things if the child has limited language.
- Ensure the new family knows what to do to console and comfort the child.

● Help the current carers to enable the child to move on.

> *It's like she has to cross a bridge to get from us to them. We've given her a good send off and they're meeting her half way. If she gets stuck in the middle, there's the social workers to keep her going.*
>
> *(Foster carer, during introductions)*

There are no prescriptions about how long it takes to cross the bridge, how wide a gap it has to span, where it should be built and what materials to use, or how to make it safe. We have to know the child, to be aware of developmental issues and to learn from our own experience. And we have to be prepared to build the best bridge and negotiate the best crossing every single time.

TIP 2

Prepare the child for this move

It is a sad fact that many young adults who have spent their childhoods in care have to struggle to relate their story. They may still not comprehend fully why they came into care or be able to recall the times they moved placements or the reasons for the moves.

To move a child successfully into a permanent placement, we must have an accurate picture of what led to the child's removal from their family of origin, and we must understand the impact these and subsequent experiences have had upon them. As professionals, we are in danger of becoming so used to terms such as "abuse" and "neglect" that we may forget what they may mean to the traumatised child.

Herman (2001, p 96) writes:

> *Repeated trauma in adult life erodes the structure of the personality already formed, but repeated trauma*

> *in childhood forms and deforms the personality.*
> *The child trapped in an abusive environment is faced*
> *with formidable tasks of adaptation. (They) must*
> *find a way of preserving a sense of trust in people*
> *who are untrustworthy, safety in a situation that is*
> *unsafe, control in a situation that is terrifyingly*
> *unpredictable, power in a situation of helplessness...*
> *(they) must compensate for the failures of adult care*
> *and protection with the only means at their disposal*
> *– an immature system of psychological defences.*

Herman describes how chronic childhood abuse often takes place in a climate of terror, with parental control enforced by threats, petty rules and intermittent rewards.

In order to survive such experiences, the child has to learn a set of adaptive responses that will, in some sense, form a blueprint for how they relate to adults, until they can be helped to build healthy, lasting attachments.

Although it would be comforting to believe that children placed in foster care from abusive or neglectful backgrounds will begin to appreciate the more positive aspects of family life, the truth is that they may be subjected to several moves and more trauma before a permanent placement can be made. It is also important to remember that most abused children do not wish to be removed from their birth families in the first place – they simply wish that the abuse will stop.

Romaine *et al* (2007, p 3) reflect that:

> *Children who have been effectively separated from*
> *their birth families, and who may have experienced*
> *a number of placements, are likely to have had their*
> *sense of belonging and identity challenged and*
> *probably fragmented. Their experience can lead*

> **them to expect that all families are temporary and**
> **conditional – people you live with for a while**
> **subject to certain conditions.**

What we are therefore aiming to do during introductions is to convey to the child that this is the household that will become theirs "for ever" and that the relationships built now will continue into early adulthood and beyond.

Preparation for making the move to permanence will need to address three principal areas:

- How did I get to be where I am now?
- Who am I and where do I belong?
- How do the past and present connect with the future?

There are many excellent resources for undertaking direct work with children in order to prepare them for a move to a permanent placement. A selection of these are listed in the bibliography.

Direct work or life story work is a process, not an event

Direct work or life story work is a process that should begin as soon as a child enters the care system and long before a permanent placement is identified. Too often this work is left undone until the last moment, when introductions are looming, in order to have something to show prospective adopters.

I have seen adopters presented with beautiful life story books, which the child has had no part in compiling, so that it played no part in helping them to understand their own unique story. Far better to have a dog-eared, messy book that the child can take pride in, and that encourages them to ask questions, express emotions and put past experiences in a form that is meaningful to them. And it need not be a book. It can be a box full of labelled memorabilia – a memory box – or a large wall map with houses, people and arrows to show the moves between them, or even a roll of old wallpaper, which one boy enthusiastically unrolled for his new family.

Argent (2006, p 13) writes:

> *Life story work is more than putting a chronological narrative together in a book and it is not the same as a photograph album with captions. It is a process that enables children to make sense of who they are and why they are where they are and to understand where they might be going. The aim of life story work must be to put their lives together again with space for the future.*

And that space includes the introductions to permanence.

Many social workers put a great deal of effort into tracking down items and photographs that will have meaning for the child, if not at the present time, then in the future. These might include a photograph of the hospital the child was born in, items of clothing, a toy that a relative wanted the child to have, and so on.

Birth relatives who are angry and upset during care proceedings are sometimes more willing to provide photographs or family information if they can be assured that the benefit will be for the child and not for the social worker. It is important to retain copies of photographs or documents in case they get lost or children destroy them. Direct work is stressful for both children and workers. If foster carers are included, they will be able to better support the child; social workers should have access to skilled supervision.

Take time to find out and answer the child's questions

As introductions approach, the child's readiness to move again has to be most carefully assessed. It is no good hoping that all will be well because we have found the "right" family at last. If the child is not emotionally ready to take the next step, the placement will be put at risk. One of the most frequent causes of disruption, revealed at disruption meetings, is the unreadiness or the reluctance of the child to move. Children may need more time to separate or they may not be ready to deal with the concept of permanence. But if children are too eager to move, this may also be a danger signal – it may indicate a lack of engagement with the present and therefore an inability to invest in the future. The child who moves without a backward glance is likely to provoke a disruption. A fair degree of apprehension is a healthier sign.

When children move, they must be helped to think about, and ask questions about, their new family. This is an opportunity for the child to air any anxieties they may still have, even if they are ready for the move. Apart from needing to know who is in their new family and where and how they live, children also seek answers to more personal questions.

- Will they know what to do if I get sick again?
- Will they leave the door open/the light on at night?
- Will I have to eat brussel sprouts?
- Will I still see my foster family/siblings/friends?
- How will I keep in touch with my mum if she doesn't write?
- What will happen if I wet the bed?
- Will they shout if I'm naughty?
- If they don't like me, where will they send me?
- If I don't like them, will I have to stay?

Every child will have his or her own list in mind; it is our job not only to listen, but also to hear what isn't said. Having their questions answered can make children feel that they are partners in this great venture, and if they feel that they are partners, then older children in particular will be more ready to invest in the success of the placement.

Holly was 12 years old. Introductions were arranged for her to meet three different families before she decided that adoption was not for her. She said she was tired of being delivered like a parcel and she preferred to stay in her residential home.

Ryan was also 12. He was a bright boy and determined to get the best out of life. He wanted a family to help him succeed. His social worker involved him in every stage of planning for permanence. When Ryan was introduced to "his" family, he decided it would do. Unlike Holly, he was able to make a conscious investment in his future.

Edith Nicholls' book, *The New Life Work Model*, offers a practical section on how foster carers can also help children to prepare for introductions (2005, p 164). Her tips include:

- Starting a "Moving On" book, which includes photographs of the new family, the new home and the area they live in, as well as names, addresses and photos of the home and people they will leave behind.
- Recording anecdotes and stories about things the child has done to share with the new family.
- Devising a planner of waiting time and agreed visits and letting the child mark off each day.
- With the child's permission, starting to pack their personal belongings in specially provided and attractive luggage, preferably chosen by the child, so that they can take some of their things each time they visit the new family.

The foster carer and social worker should also make time to look at, and talk about, the book or video or any other materials the new family have made for the child. This is discussed in greater detail in Tip 7.

Good practice points

- Make sure that sufficient time has been made available to undertake direct work with the child. The social worker must be responsible for the formal work to prepare the child for introductions, but foster carers should be aware that much informal life story work is part of day-to-day living. Giving attention, sharing activities and building trust will help the child to form a positive personal narrative and so be receptive to plans for their future.

- Remember that direct work is never ending and will be continued by the new family into permanent placement.
- Acknowledge and encourage the child to talk about all their feelings in connection with an impending move.
- Offer reassurance that it is quite normal to feel anxious or apprehensive when faced with something new.
- Understand that all moves involve endings and losses, and that when children have been traumatised, all transitions may be traumatic and all endings destructive.

TIP 3

Prepare the family for the impact of introductions

> *It's surreal – being introduced to your son – there's no other words to describe it. I felt like I'd pass out with the tension and the emotion of it.*
>
> *(Adopter of a three-year-old)*

A vital part of the success of any placement is ensuring that adopters have had full background information about the child or children the agency is hoping to place with them. It is crucial that all the information contained in the Child Permanence Report or Form E and all other relevant records, and the implications for them as a family, both now and in the future, are fully discussed well before introductions begin. The actual period of introductions is usually intense and should focus only on the reality of what is going on and the feelings that are engendered.

If prospective carers have had a thorough training, if they have participated in a "joint" assessment, if they have been pro-active in identifying a specific child or children and have been provided with all available background information, then they will be able to draw on their knowledge during introductions. It may be necessary to refer them back in terms of 'Remember when we talked about…', but the preparation for permanence is over and they have to take that leap into the dark. That is how one adoptive father described introductions.

> *You learn all there is to learn about adoption, and you discover a lot about yourself, and you read and hear all there is to know about this child. But when it comes to it, when you go to that first meeting, you're still taking a leap into the dark.*

There is then, perhaps, still a need for that extra bit of preparation for that "leap into the dark" – for the introductions that are like no others. It may help adopters to steady their nerves if they take time to consider:

- What might the child be feeling at this point?
- What kind of feelings and behaviour might they expect the child to display during the first meeting and how might this change over the course of introductions? It is important for adopters to understand that children who have settled well in foster homes may revert to previous behaviour when they are moved again.
- What questions might the child ask?
- What would upset them/please them during introductions? What is their dream scenario?
- How might the foster carers be feeling at this point?
- What will be this child's needs during introductions?

● Is there any information about the child they would like to discuss
  further? It often happens that adopters do not "hear" difficult
  stories in their eagerness to have a child.

Meeting other people

Adopters/permanent carers will need to be introduced to key people
in a child's life in order to gain a realistic picture of what living with
the child is like on a day-to-day basis. A meeting with the current
foster carer has to be the first step. It may require more than one visit
to establish a co-operative relationship and much will depend on this
rapport. A smooth transition is rarely achieved if the two sets of carers
do not approve of each other. And disapproval may be open or covert
– either way, it can undermine a placement and damage the child.

> *I knewed my foster mum didn't like them 'cause she
> never gave them a cup of tea or nothing. So I didn't
> like them neither.*
>
> (Child of seven, after failed introductions)

Foster carers require training to let children go with a blessing, and
adopters have to develop greater appreciation of the foster carers'
task. Any time invested in this part of the process is time well spent,
even if it delays the first meeting. One single adopter at first felt
intimidated by the infant's experienced foster carer, but in the end
she was grateful to her for handing over a 'perfect, healthy baby in
a settled routine and already sleeping through the night'. The carer
remained a supportive friend of the new family.

Access to the agency's medical adviser allows the adopters to talk
over all medical information and to gain an understanding of what
particular aspects of the child's history might mean in the future, for
example, where there are concerns about parental drug or alcohol
misuse, mental health or hereditary conditions. Health visitors can fill
in the developmental details about a young child, especially if the child
has any degree of disability or requires special treatment.

It is always helpful for prospective adopters to speak to the teachers of school-age children and to see for themselves the environment where the child has spent a great deal of time. School may be as significant as the foster home, and will certainly be compared by the child with the next one.

Consideration should also be given to holding a Life Appreciation Day shortly before introductions begin. This provides an opportunity for adopters/permanent carers to meet people who have known or worked with the child, and provides a forum for an exchange of anecdotes, videos and photographs to present a multi-faceted view of the child. Anyone who has a story to tell can be included. A foster carer's neighbour or the parent of a school friend may be able to add to the picture. The social workers involved can provide prepared visual material, such as flipcharts with family circles, family trees and charts to illustrate the child's history of achievements, moves and losses. Many adopters welcome this guided journey through a child's life and feel that it prepares them to meet the real child better than all the reports they have read. A Life Appreciation Day works best in informal and comfortable surroundings with biscuits, hot drinks and sandwiches laid on for lunch.

Good practice points

- Check and double-check that all information about the child has been fully shared. Consider the use of an Information Sharing Checklist or similar device.
- Enable adopters to think about the needs of the child during introductions.
- If there are gaps in the information, acknowledge what these are.
- Give the adopters time to meet key people in the child's life prior to introductions.
- Offer a Life Appreciation Day and be prepared to devote the whole day to it.
- Encourage prospective carers to consider the impact they will have on the child and the impact this child will have on them when they meet.

The devil truly is in the detail when making permanent placements; our responsibility is to ensure that people have all the available information on which they can base informed decisions, and that they are fully prepared to take the next step at each stage.

TIP 4

Focus on the child or children

Children and adopters need to practise being together, but children also need to learn how to separate from current carers. For the adopter or permanent carer, introductions are an opportunity to practise, perhaps for the first time, being a parent, or certainly being a parent to this child or sibling group. Children will discover what it will be like to be looked after by these people and will begin to make comparisons between these and previous carers.

It is important during introductions for children to have as much time as practicable with the adopters, at different times of the day, so that the new parents can learn the children's routines, preferences, strengths and difficulties. This, in time, will make children feel confident that these new people will be able to cope, and that it is safe to cross the bridge from foster care to adoption. If, for example, the child is particularly difficult to settle at bedtime, this is an ideal time for the adopters to see how the foster carer manages, and to gain experience in settling the child.

It is very important that introductions are not cluttered with treats and events that get in the way of the children and adults spending ordinary time together. Family life is built on the repetition of day-to-day activities, such as shopping, going to the local park, cooking meals and eating together. It is quite special enough to be introduced to someone who will be your parent – no other excitement is required.

Schofield and Beek (2007, p 235) have identified some principles which apply to sensitive practice and which are useful to bear in mind during introductions. These include:

- Offering a secure base – this can be promoted by the child seeing the foster carer and the new family co-operating. On a practical level, this should mean that introductions move from the carer's home to the new home with both sets of adults fully involved. It helps if the child can help pack their things for the move with the foster carer and adopter together. This allows for dialogue about items that may have special memories or value for the child.
- Having a social worker who is known and trusted by the child – this helps to build that vital bridge between one placement and another by creating a sense of continuity for the child.
- Helping children to regulate their feelings in the heightened emotional state engendered by introductions– this means spending more time with each child.
- It goes without saying that children's belongings should never be packed into bin bags – this is not the message we want to give!
- Working with the child to feel effective – children who have grown up in the care system often say that they felt powerless, that they were moved around by the system and felt they had no control over, or say in, what happened to them. We can avoid this by consulting with children over the introduction plan according to their age and understanding.
- Family membership – it is easy to overlook how bewildering and disorientating a move to a new home can be for a child, even if routines remain the same as far as possible.

We must not forget that every household has different "rules" and expectations and that these will have to be explained over and over again to a child joining the family. For example, some families always eat at a table whilst others tend to have meals in front of the TV. Some families would expect an older child to ask for something from the fridge, whilst others don't mind if the children help themselves. In some homes it is all right to flush the toilet in the night, but in other homes it is not. These are just some of the rules adopted children might have to learn, and there are many more. This was brought home very powerfully to one adoptive mum who told her seven-year-old to get a spoon for her yoghurt, at which point the little girl burst into tears, saying, 'But I don't even know where the spoons in this house are!'

We only have to remind ourselves how strange it can feel when we go and stay in an unfamiliar environment while on holiday or with a friend or relative for a few days. Imagine then how overwhelming it could be for a small child to be placed in strange surroundings. The new family can promote a sense of belonging by explaining, literally, 'this is how we do things around here'. Such simple things as giving older children a say in how to lay out their room or where to keep their things can help. One set of adopters had a personalised wooden name plaque made for a six-year-old's bedroom, which they put up together on the day she moved in.

Good practice points

- Use introductions to create opportunities to "practise".
- Don't plan lots of treats – plan mundane everyday family things to do together.
- Find ways to familiarise the child with the new home.
- Promote co-operation between all the adults involved in introductions.
- Maintain as much continuity as possible during every transition.

> *My social worker was "there" for me. All the time when my new family turned up and I had to leave my other foster place, she was "there" for me, seeing me off safe, like.*
>
> (Boy in permanent foster home)

TIP 5

Introducing siblings

> *From the moment we met the three of them, we felt overpowered by their demands, by their aggression to each other, but also by their obvious hunger for love.*
>
> *(Adopter after meeting three siblings under five)*

It makes huge demands on social workers to place siblings. They must work with each child separately, as well as assessing them as part of a sibling group. Far-reaching decisions about placing them together or apart have to be reached long before they are linked with families. And then there are no short cuts to getting to know the children before they are introduced to prospective permanent carers.

Points to consider

- How does the group deal with stress in the family? How do the siblings deal with conflict within the group? How does each child react to pressure?
- Do siblings recognise each other's distress and comfort each other?
- Do they close rank against outsiders?
- Do they forgive each other for real or imagined transgressions?
- Does any one child take responsibility, or blame, for the actions of all?
- Can each child express feelings, wishes and opinions or is there a spokesperson?
- Is play boisterous and pleasurable or competitive and aggressive?
- Which children "gang up", "pair off", or appear to be "loners"?
- How and to whom do individual children show affection?
- Does one child "wind the others up" or get them into trouble?
- Who shares and who does not?
- Who copies whom and how do siblings describe each other?
- How does each child rank in the sibling group and gain the attention of adults?

(Adapted from *Ten Top Tips on Placing Siblings*, Argent, 2008)

The answers to all these questions will have an impact on how the introductions should be planned and managed for a sibling group, and also give rise to further deliberations.

If several children are to be placed together, should they be introduced and placed one at a time or all at the same time? There is something to be said for "serial" placements that follow the more usual way to build a family.

Perhaps very large sibling groups could join their new family in pairs – this gives more time and space for preparation and for initial relationships to be made. But this approach has to be balanced against the resentment and heightened sibling rivalry established children and newcomers might feel towards each other.

Decisions depending on circumstances will have to be made if siblings are being placed together at the same time: should each child spend some time alone with each and with both parents during introductions?

If brothers and sisters who have been separated are to be reunited, should this happen for a period before introductions begin, so that they can rebuild their relationships without simultaneously having to adjust to a "forever" family?

Whichever model for placing a sibling group is chosen, the children need to be involved in the decisions, so that they will be able to understand, according to age and ability, the aims and purpose of the introductions.

One local authority found a family to take five siblings aged between four and 11 who had been placed in a residential home together. The children were introduced to the new family as a group; they got to know the family and their home and even knew exactly where they would sleep. They were all included in the planning and review of introductions, and agreed that the oldest should move in first so that she could 'help the others to settle because she would know her way around'. The remaining siblings made frequent visits to their new home and helped to get their rooms ready until the middle two moved in together. The two youngest joined them six weeks later after several overnight stays.

These children all felt part of a special placement project. The oldest child had always been burdened with responsibility for her brothers and sisters and was able to respond to the attention she was given, while helping to plan for her siblings' arrival. The middle two children, who were twins, had a spell of being the oldest and then the youngest, which they made the most of, and the youngest children felt safe immediately when they joined their older sisters and brothers again. The adopters always felt in control, which also made the children feel secure.

However, this cannot be a model to fit all large sibling groups. There is no substitute for assessing each case separately, no matter what the similarities. The more children there are in a group, the more complex the questions and the decisions about how they should be introduced and placed. But the aims of introductions must remain the same: to make children and families feel comfortable enough with each other to want to live together.

Good practice points

- Take time to get to know each child and the dynamics of the sibling group before any decisions about introductions are made.
- Work with each child separately and also as part of a group when preparing them for introductions.
- Be flexible during introductions and placement, particularly if a large sibling group is being placed: consider "serial" placements or placing children in pairs rather than as one group.
- Consider each child's needs separately and as a group: should each child spend time alone with their new carers/parents during introductions? Should separated brothers and sisters be reunited before introductions begin?
- Remember, every introduction of a sibling group will be different, and the more children involved, the more complex the questions and decisions will be.

TIP 6

Consider the birth family

> *The minute Alan's birth father walked into the room, I could see that he was Alan's father. It was quite uncanny, the sort of resemblance, I guess, that "normal" families take for granted. I discovered that he had been a talented sportsman before he was ill...I wondered if Alan would go on to be a sporty type like his father... Now, several years on, I believe he will.*
>
> (Wise, 2007, p 72)

The purpose of a meeting with birth parents can be:

- to set the scene for future contact, either direct or indirect letter box contact;
- to allow the most important people in the child's life to meet and

to forge some sort of understanding of one another.

> *I think my life is easier for me because my mum and my parents are in contact. They write letters to each other. My parents think my mum is a very nice person. If they didn't write I'd feel upset because I'd think they didn't like each other and were jealous of each other.*
>
> *(Georgie, aged 11, quoted in Harris, 2008, p 133)*

Meeting birth parents

Meeting the birth parents can have a profound effect on adopters. They may fear that a meeting will disrupt placement plans, but these fears are almost always unfounded. On the whole, birth parents do not want to distress their children. In her study of birth relatives who have face-to-face contact with their adopted children, Neil (2003) found that uppermost in the minds of many was their wish not to cause any upset or make any demands. Many carers find it hard to envisage the birth parents as people other than linked to the circumstances that led to the child being permanently taken away from them. Some adopters have truthfully said that they expected to dislike the birth parents prior to meeting them, but that they came away with a better "feel" for them and a greater understanding, and that nothing short of meeting the birth mother could have dispelled the threatening fantasy.

> *When the moment comes, I'm within an inch of saying I can't go through with it. But in the end I do. We have been plied with so much discouraging information that it is fair to say we are not at all keen to meet her. The meeting is fairly short and Peter's mother is as nice as could be. My heart goes out to her and all I want to do is hug her...She is*

> *very young and immature and quiet...At the end of the meeting we have our photo taken together for Peter's life story book and we promise to maintain letterbox contact once a year with photos included.*
>
> *(James, 2006, p 84)*

Sometimes a meeting has made adopters realise that birth parents could still make a meaningful contribution to their children's lives. It certainly makes letterbox contact more significant if both senders know whom they are writing to. At the very least, a meeting can enable parents to tell their adopted children about it when they begin to ask questions about their birth parents.

> *She was a sad person, with a sad background. I felt great sympathy for her...there was something about her that reminded me of Alan, though. He had her smile, her laugh and the same expression in his eyes – yes, these were the positive things I would be able to tell Alan when he wanted to know the details.*
>
> *(Wise, 2007, p 71)*

Meeting other birth family members

It isn't only birth parents who may have something to contribute to a permanent placement. Grandparents in particular, and also adult siblings, can fill in gaps and can often give a more rounded picture of the child's background. It will depend on the circumstances of each case whether adopters meet birth family members all together or one at a time.

> *Alan's birth grandmother was a very nice, ordinary woman, not too much older than me! She had been*

> *very ill, which was one of the reasons, she*
> *explained, that she and her husband had not been*
> *able to consider having Alan...She told me that she*
> *too, had been adopted as a baby and that she had*
> *discovered it by chance aged 16...She urged me*
> *always to tell Alan the truth, because the lies can*
> *never be forgotten.*
>
> *(Wise, 2007, p 72)*

Points to consider

Points to consider when planning meetings between adopters and birth parents include the following:

- It is important that adopters have a "breathing space" after meeting the birth family and do not have to go on to other meetings the same day.
- It is usually not advisable to add to the emotional charge by meeting the birth family members during introductions – just before is better.
- Arrival at the venue should be carefully planned so that the prospective carers and birth family do not meet in the car park or on the doorstep first.
- A single birth parent should be invited to bring a relative or friend, particularly if they are meeting a couple.
- Such meetings often work best if the birth parents leave the meeting first, accompanied by whoever is supporting them. They should be offered a lift home if they have no transport.

Preparation

Birth family members will need careful preparation for meeting the adopters and support from someone they trust – perhaps a family centre worker or someone from another agency. This should, of course, be part of the ongoing work with the birth family, which means that they will already have been given basic information about the new family and about the placement plan, and will have been involved in agreeing contact arrangements. They also need to be prepared for how long the meeting will last and what questions they might want to raise.

The person entrusted with preparing the birth family also needs to think about what boundaries to impose on birth parents who misuse drugs or alcohol. For some people it may be a chronic problem and it may be unrealistic to insist that they come to a meeting totally drug- or alcohol-free. But it also needs to be made clear that the meeting cannot go ahead if someone is incoherent, aggressive or behaving erratically. Even people with an entrenched problem can respect this as a ground rule.

Most birth family members who are still very angry with social services because their child has been compulsorily removed, reserve their anger for social work staff or the court, and are often glad to have the opportunity to meet the person or people who are to be parenting their child.

It is helpful for birth parents to think specifically of what they want their child to know about them so that adopters/permanent carers can tell the child in the future. This might include any interests they have, what hopes they have for the child, for themselves and so on. Birth parents sometimes bring photographs of other family members along, which can provide an easy talking point and lead into family anecdotes.

It is important to find a safe, informal venue, and preferably not one that holds upsetting memories for the birth family (e.g. a social services meeting room!). Refreshments, easy chairs and a private room help to create the right atmosphere.

The meeting

It is useful to begin the meeting with the social worker thanking everyone for coming and saying that this is an opportunity to talk about anything the child's birth mother or father would like to share with the adopters. Most birth parents will want to convey that they loved their child and will look for reassurance that the child will be told this.

Workers need to be prepared for the fact that this can be an emotional meeting for both birth parents and families. It should be kept fairly short with tissues at the ready!

Birth family members will need time and the opportunity to "de-brief" with their social workers very soon after the meeting. The prospective adopters are likely to feel a range of emotions following the meeting, which may include sadness about what the birth parents have lost and guilt about "taking" their child away. They should be reassured that these feelings are very normal. They should also feel heartened that often the success of these meetings can lay the foundation for positive post-placement contact.

Good practice points

- Prepare both birth family members and adopters/permanent carers for the meeting.
- Identify a safe and comfortable venue that allows for privacy.
- Include the extended birth family whenever appropriate.
- Allow both parties time to de-brief after the meeting.
- If everyone agrees, take photographs that can be put into the child's life story book.

> *She's got loads of photos of her birth mum, who sends them to her every year. She doesn't bother with them much, but the one she really likes, and she has it framed by her bed, is the one of us and her mum together.*
>
> *(Adoptive mother of teenager)*

TIP 7

Clear the decks!

We have to ensure that key people in the child's life are not distracted by other commitments or demands on their time when introductions are going on. Everyone has to be focused on the forthcoming task and must be prepared to place the child's needs firmly at the centre. We cannot assume that introductions will always go smoothly, but we can give this process the best possible chance of success by making child-centred plans.

For the social workers concerned, this means making sure that they are not on leave, or due to be in court for care proceedings just before, during, or after introductions, or that they have any commitments that cannot be altered. Carers and other people involved should not have booked holidays or activities that could affect the length or scope of introductions. One adoptive parent blamed serious problems in a placement on rushed introductions that had to be fitted around a foster carer's planned admission to hospital. She said the child had never separated properly from the carer or connected with them – she was still hovering in the middle.

Although foster carers may look forward to having a holiday immediately after a child leaves, it is a good idea to postpone it for a little while: introductions may not go quite according to plan, and in most cases foster carers can give invaluable support in the early days of a placement. We also need to check what care commitments the foster family has at this time. Is there, for example, a heavy schedule of contact for another child in the placement? How will this be managed?

Support leading up to introductions

The child's social worker will have a pivotal role in talking to the child, the foster carer and the prospective family during the time leading up to introductions. She or he must judge what, if anything, may need to be talked about or decided before introductions can begin. For example, what does the child want to call the adopters? What do the adopters want to be called? Older children can be encouraged to choose an attractive notebook in which to write down (with the help of their foster carer if necessary) any questions they may have about their new parents and their family. This also helps the family to understand what the child may be concerned about.

The importance of different regional accents, words, and culture should not be overlooked.

> *Two young children being placed in an inter-agency arrangement came from north-east England and moved to London. They and the adopters had many different words for things, their accents were very broad and they literally could not understand each other. These children also thought they had moved abroad, because they came on a plane.*

Maps of the UK showing where people live, and how far away from each other, are useful preparation tools.

The foster carers will have started talking to the child or children about the impending move and sharing information about the new family, perhaps in the form of a DVD or a book. Here are some other inventive ways of introducing the family to the child before the first meeting.

- A pin board to hang up in the child's room/living space in the foster home, with photos and messages from family to child.
- A placemat (laminated) with photos of the prospective family for use at mealtimes, to generate discussion about life with the new family.
- An infant's toy (perhaps a rattle) with laminated photo(s) of the new carer(s).
- Playing with dolls/doll houses to enact stories about families and children moving to new families.

It is advisable for the child to have had a settled period in the run-up to introductions, so it would be unwise to plan for the process to begin immediately after, say, a family holiday with the foster carers or a spell of respite care.

The foster carers are expected, at this time, to be very giving of themselves both emotionally and physically. But they also have a legitimate interest in minimising the disruption to their own families when a foster child leaves. Any other foster children or birth children will need support in the run-up to, as well as during, introductions, and it is vital for the supervising social worker to be available for this task.

Most foster carers want the introductions to go well, but they need practical as well as emotional help to allow them to concentrate on the child. If introductions are to involve having the new family in their home for hours at a time, as well as requiring them to travel to the new home, it is imperative that financial help with transport, reimbursement for extra food, and assistance with arrangements for other foster children are agreed before the introductions begin. It is hard for foster carers to be enthusiastic about a move if they have to worry about how much it is costing them and whether they will have the time to fit everything in.

The adopters/permanent carers are likely to feel both nervous and apprehensive at this point. They are about to embark on a journey which may ultimately involve parenting a child they don't yet know and with whom they have no shared history. They may worry about "getting it wrong" during introductions and they will be aware that their display of parenting skills will be under scrutiny – skills they may not yet have and will have to learn. This is the time for reassurance to boost their confidence. Families can make the most of this waiting time by exploring local resources for their child-to-be, such as play groups, or educational, medical and leisure services.

If adopters/permanent carers work outside the home, they will need to think about getting adoption leave or taking annual leave to free them from outside pressures. They will also need to be reminded that introductions are a time when they will be getting to know their child and that, for now, they will have to ask their extended family and friends to remain in the background. The new family's task is to form a relationship with the child, and this is made far more difficult if well-meaning relatives and friends keep popping around or phoning up at inopportune moments! One way around this is for the adopters/permanent carers to contact one person in their network regularly who can then report to the others.

Money matters should also be discussed and confirmed before introductions are planned. If there is to be an adoption allowance, assessments should have been completed by this stage and payment methods agreed. Is a "settling-in" grant available? Some agencies will pay for furniture, prams and other necessary equipment. It is not a good idea to leave this until the introductions planning meeting, as this could be embarrassing for families and distract from the purpose of the meeting. Will adopters' expenses for introductions be covered?

By this time, contact arrangements with the birth family should have been negotiated and agreed. However, it may be helpful for workers to encourage adopters to discuss any concerns they may have.

Wisdom gleaned from practice

- Avoid introductions at Christmas, birthdays or during other festivities – these are emotionally loaded and busy times when life is far from normal. Most people do more socialising, shopping and eating than usual, and family gatherings are also notorious for producing family tensions. Everyday life is what the child and the new parents should be practising.
- Avoid times when familiar people are away, e.g. a favourite person

in the foster family or one of the social workers.

- Avoid times when adult agendas would have to dictate the pace of introductions. Adopters and carers who are worried about taking time off work, or about the illness of a close family member or friend, or a foster carer with builders in the house, are not going to be able to completely focus on the task.

- Think carefully about timings during school holidays. Whilst the long holidays can be a good time for unhurried introductions, it can be very daunting for a new parent and child to face six unbroken weeks of summer without a break when they are just trying to get to know one another. One placement disrupted very quickly because the adopter felt she had to fill six weeks with daily excursions, outings and "treats", which she then found exhausting and unrewarding, as did the child. Sometimes moves towards the end of the long holidays work well, to allow the new parent and child to prepare for the new school together.

- It is easier to join a class at the beginning of term than in mid–term when friendships have been established. A new child often attracts a lot of questions, which they should be equipped to answer. 'What will you say if people ask…?' should be part of life story work in preparation for permanent placement.

What is vital is that we are aware how tricky and complex the planning of introductions can be, and that we do not seek to impose an unworkable schedule on any of the people involved.

Good practice points

- Ensure that key people are available during the whole of the period of introductions and are not distracted by other events.
- Do not allow introductions to be led by an adult agenda.
- Have someone itemise in advance any commitments that cannot be altered and which could impact on the timings of introductions.
- Ensure that foster carers are well supported both emotionally and practically during the time leading up to introductions.
- Consider timings carefully – avoid "emotionally loaded" events.
- Ensure that the child's needs are central at all times.

> *Eleven-year-old Lily was distraught when she was told that she would miss the last day of school. The class had been working on a "Black British" project, which was to culminate in a carnival parade and she would have to miss it when she went to meet her new family.*
>
> *(Argent, 2006, p 44)*

How easily this problem could have been avoided if Lily's needs had been made paramount.

TIP 8

Agree an introduction plan – but don't write it in stone

Once any constraints have been identified and overcome, you are ready to move to planning the introductions proper.

> *While the shared hope is that a placement will be made, the reality is that introductions provide the opportunity for the child and family to learn more about each other. Introductions are not irrevocable and all involved need explicit permission to share reservations so that concerns can be worked with.*
>
> (Byrne, 2002, p 10)

The introductions planning meeting

Byrne (2000, p 30) has reproduced an excellent sample agenda for the introductions planning meeting (see Appendix). One of the helpful suggestions is that participants at the meeting be given a suitable summary of the key points for either verbal or pre-verbal children from Vera Fahlberg's *A Child's Journey Through Placement* (1994, p 198), entitled 'Moving a child to adoption'.

The foster carers, adopters/permanent carers, social workers from each agency (if it is an inter-agency placement) and their managers should attend, and there will need to be agreement about the agenda, who is to chair the meeting and how minutes will be taken to record decisions.

Many agencies use the BAAF *Form H* for this meeting, and the person chairing should ensure that the form has been partially completed, prior to the meeting, with the key known facts such as the date of the placement order or its equivalent. This is to avoid undue delay whilst files are rifled through to gather basic information that could easily have been documented before the meeting began.

Everyone should be given daily timetable sheets to work on, but it is best if the Chair completes them and distributes copies at the end of the meeting, so that everyone has the same details written down. Introductions planning meetings can quickly develop into disarray if people jot down their own version of what they think they have agreed!

The Chair should check and note that the prospective carers have had, in writing, all the recorded information pertaining to the child and that they are satisfied with the contents. The foster carers should have provided, also in writing, details of the child's routines and anything else they consider the family should know.

The prospective carers should confirm that they have had a chance to meet previously with the foster carers and the birth family as well as the agency medical adviser, the child's teachers or child minder and health visitor.

The Chair should also check that life story work has been undertaken and that it is ready to go with the child. It should also be confirmed that statutory notifications about the move will be sent to the relevant agencies as detailed in *Form H*.

Everyone should be reminded of what the introductions plan is meant to achieve. Writing the main points on a flip chart can help to focus the minds of the group:

- Introductions should enable the child or children to move from one set of carers to another.
- Introductions should enable children and new families to practise being together.
- By the end of introductions, the new carers should feel confident about each child's day-to-day routines.
- Introductions should familiarise children to their new surroundings.

A pictorial representation of the bridge between the two families that the child has to cross can add to the understanding.

Practicalities

Time must be given to discuss practicalities. If families have to stay away from home during introductions, where will that be and who will make the arrangements? Accommodation should be convenient and comfortable. It can be very hard to come back to a miserable, cold room after an emotional day. The same applies for foster carers if they are to stay near the new family's home for the last part of introductions.

It will help the child to settle into their new home if everything of importance such as favourite toys, bedding and clothes can go to the new home with them. Any items that the foster carer has been given for the child by the birth parents should be passed on and their significance explained. Suitcases should be purchased for the move if not already provided.

Transport to fit in with the introduction plan must be agreed. Children and carers will be tense enough without added anxiety about travel.

Support and communication

- Support for all parties during introductions is essential and it is good practice to circulate a sheet containing everyone's land and mobile phone numbers. All parties should also have the telephone number of the Emergency Duty Team.

- All parties will need to be seen by their social worker during introductions and visits should be agreed at this meeting.
- If more than one child is being introduced, it is essential that their individual needs and reactions are closely monitored.
- One worker, usually the child's, should liaise with all others to monitor the progress of introductions after every scheduled meeting.
- Stressing the importance of having one named person responsible for overseeing the introductions, with whom any changes should be agreed, also emphasises that no alterations to the plan should be made unilaterally but that everything is open to further discussion.
- Timing of telephone contact should be agreed at the meeting in order to avoid unnecessary frustration.
- A document about sharing parental responsibility with the new family should have been drawn up and presented at panel when the match was agreed. The Chair of the meeting should offer a timely reminder of "who decides what" during introductions.
- Children with sensory impairments may need special aids to communication. They may have to become familiar with new people and new surroundings by using their sense of smell and touch.

Natalie was blind. Her prospective carers always wore the same clothes and watches and jewellery during introductions; the same scent and aftershave lotion. They always brought the same audiotape to play to her and when introductions moved to the new home, the clothes and smells and sounds came too.

(Argent, 2006, p 46)

We have to be aware not only of children's special needs but also of the needs of the adopters. Single people may require more regular support from their social worker during introductions in order to discuss progress, or they may choose to include a close relative or friend in some visits. If different cultures or ethnicities are involved, we must be careful to respect customs and traditions: language, clothes, food and religious festivals may have to be considered when the introduction plan is made.

Other children

It is vital to decide exactly whether, and how and when, other foster children, carers' or adopters' own children should be involved in introductions. Much will, of course, depend on age and understanding.

It makes sense for other children not to be present when the new family meets the child for the first time. Apart from being a distraction for all concerned, birth children should not be involved in the decision to go ahead or not to go ahead, any more than if their parents were thinking about producing a biological sibling.

If other children at both ends of the transitional bridge have been well prepared for the loss or addition to their family, they will be able to accept a plan that includes them at appropriate points.

For an older birth child, spending time in a foster carer's home can be boring and stressful unless there are other foster children of a similar age. Thought needs to be given to how siblings-to-be can spend time together during introductions in an enjoyable way. It is important that birth children retain their routine and special time with their parents.

> *During one set of introductions, a nine-year-old birth child asked if he and his parents could have a one-day break so it could be just the three of them before the new child joined the family. By giving him this, his parents were able to reassure him that he would always have a special place in the family.*

Meetings and visits

The first few meetings with the child must take place in the foster carers' home and it should be agreed how and when the new family can begin to take over key tasks with the child – feeding, bathing and taking the child out on their own for brief periods. How many visits this takes and the frequency of the visits will vary according to the child's age and the family's experience and confidence. This is not an easy stage of the process. Children hardly ever want to sit quietly to meet visitors or to have a chat. Any ordinary domestic activity, game or local outing will enable children and adults to be together and to observe each other. The very first meeting with the child should be kept quite short and arranged for a time when the child will not be tired or hungry or wanting to be somewhere else, like at football club or ballet class.

Usually the child's social worker is present at the first meeting; their role is to encourage the two families to discuss the child's routine and to encourage the adopters/permanent carers to engage with the child. It is important that the adopters do not feel they have "failed" if the child does not immediately take an interest in them. It is equally important that they do not overwhelm the child with interest – some children are very reticent while others will make a beeline for attentive adults.

It is advisable to steer clear of saying something along the lines of 'This is your new mummy and daddy', and to let children decide what to call the adopters – if anything. What is important is that the child sees that these are people to be trusted and that this message is reinforced by the foster carer both verbally and non-verbally.

The current carers should go along on the first outing with the new family in order to make the child feel secure and to demonstrate their approval. Next time the child may be brave enough to go out without them.

The prospective family should stay locally if they live too far away to make frequent journeys without undue wear and tear. On days when they do not visit, they should telephone the child and foster family or post cards to arrive on the right days.

After the visits to the foster home, ideally there should be an "about-turn", and the process of familiarisation should continue on the new family's patch. This time, the foster carer will be on strange ground and will help the child to get to know more about the new family, the new surroundings, the new home, perhaps the new school. The foster carer should then withdraw as carefully as the new family takes over, by leaving the child for longer periods each time. Overnight stays should be introduced during this stage, during which some of the child's belongings can be gradually transferred. Birth children should be included in the arrangements whenever possible.

The foster carers should be accommodated locally if they live too far away to manage the journey frequently – some foster carers use the opportunity to have a family holiday if there is an attractive place nearby. This also preserves continuity for other foster children, with the reassurance that no one has disappeared.

A date, time and venue to review the introductions should be agreed – this is generally about mid-way through, but it is better if the child will have been introduced to the new family's home so that their readiness for the move will be more apparent. Participants should be warned that the date might be changed if there are concerns about the placement proceeding.

Every detail of the introduction plan should be entered on the time sheets. The plan should cover everything from the precise arrangements for the first meeting to the placement itself, with all the visits and phone calls and postcards in between.

Good practice points

- Decide who is to chair and who is to minute the introductions planning meeting.
- Agree an agenda.
- Circulate the extract 'Helping children when they must move' to participants in advance.
- Make sure everyone has the same timetable sheets.
- If there are geographical considerations, ensure accommodation has been booked for the adopters and the foster carers.
- Consider the needs of foster children and birth children as well as those of the child in transition.

- Agree the date and place for the review of introductions.
- Circulate telephone numbers and ensure people know who they can talk to in case of difficulty.
- Make sure the plan is agreed by all – imposed plans can come unstuck!
- Agree that social workers will check in with everyone before and after every meeting – even if things are going extremely well.
- Don't bank on instant success, but expect the unexpected.

> *When I remember that moment, in my heart it's like one of those romantic wedding pictures that you see, where a couple are in the centre of the picture and they're framed by a sort of blurry mist of time or whatever. The truth is, that he came running to the door, with something horrible and sticky all round his mouth and his nappy, a frankly rather stinky one, was hanging off him. Somehow, although it must have registered somewhere in my memory, I didn't notice that at the time. Love at first sight? Yes, I think so.*
>
> (Wise, 2007, p 55)

TIP 9

See how it goes and go at the child's pace

> *You have to get used to the home, have to get used to where you live and the places outside. It's not what you're used to. Your next-door neighbours. You have to get used to everything really.*
>
> (Child of 12, quoted in Thomas et al, 1999, p 59)

Just as there is no clear-cut division between life stages, so there is no clear-cut break between introductions, placement, legal adoption and life after adoption or permanent placement. With the right decisions and good management, one stage simply flows into the next. Practising to live together goes on when children move in for good with their new families. Each step in the permanent placement process is a continuation from the last one, and success on the way forward will depend on the foundations laid behind.

Clear lines of communications, support and openness are the cornerstones of effective introductions.

Communications and support

- Children will feel safe if they get the message that their new family cares for their well-being and is liked and trusted by the other adults involved.
- Children in care usually have experience of being moved without much preparation or explanation, so it can be reassuring for them if their new family also gives clear messages: 'We'll come again soon' is not at all the same as 'We will collect you from school next Thursday; we will wait for you by the main gate'. Some children have bitter memories of adults who said 'See you soon', and never did.
- It is not good if the child's social worker doesn't know what went on during a weekend visit or if the new family doesn't know how the child reacted after they left the foster home. And it is no good at all if the adoption and fostering agency only knows what is going well and not what may be going badly.
- One worker should have the lead responsibility for co-ordinating introductions and monitoring progress after every scheduled meeting.
- The child's social worker will need to see the child during introductions to ascertain their feelings and wishes, and to keep them informed of any changes to the plan.
- The adopters/permanent carers should be able to meet their worker as and when needed during introductions and stay in regular telephone contact.
- The supervising social worker needs to allocate time to keep in regular touch with the foster carers.
- All parties should know whom to contact in an emergency.
- Workers should be prepared for out-of-hours contact if visits are scheduled for evenings and weekends.
- Everyone has to know which worker will be available when, and who will be supporting the child, the current carers and the

new family.

- The plan has to be constantly monitored; not everything will work out exactly as agreed.
- A review meeting at a pre-arranged point during introductions should allow all parties to be heard. The child should be represented by their social worker. If necessary, there can be more than one meeting to review progress.

Openness

At every stage of the journey to permanent placements, adopters must be given the opportunity to move on or to withdraw. By the time it gets to introductions, withdrawing becomes fraught with feelings of remorse, guilt and regret mixed with only marginal relief. But we all have to accept that it can't work every time. Only by being open can we all work towards the same end without misunderstandings and misconceptions.

- As well as helping children to move, we must pay attention to their doubts during introductions and let them know that we are listening.
- Prospective permanent carers have to know from the very beginning that introductions will not inevitably lead to placement; at the same time, introductions should be regarded as the expected step before placement and not as a "trying it out" procedure.

It was knowing that we didn't have to go on that made us persevere and get over the hump. It was really hard at times, but somehow he got under our skin and there we were, he was our son.

(Adopter, after introductions)

- It is vital that adopters should feel fully supported, and know that any concerns arising during introductions will be shared with them immediately. Naturally, their progress should also be noted.

- It is equally vital that prospective families are encouraged to raise any concerns they may have themselves.

> *This is when we begin to feel quite alarmingly out of our depth – standing in someone else's house – watching while the family goes about its routine. It is 6am, it is still dark outside, and we are not yet fully awake after an almost sleepless night.*
>
> (James, 2006, p 83)

- Foster carers must be confident that their views will be heard and respected.
- Social workers and other professionals need to share their observations, and not feel that they have to protect their own clients or fear that a "failed" introduction will reflect on their competence.
- It is essential that everyone should feel they can be open and honest about any doubts they might have.

> *One newly-qualified social worker was so anxious about his first adoption assessment that he did not tell his colleagues about the adopters' negative feelings for one of the two children. The placement went ahead as planned, but the older child was rejected after a six-month struggle, and siblings were separated.*

Making changes

However thorough the introduction meeting, and detailed the introduction plan, it can only offer a firm framework and it hardly ever remains unaltered. The venue, activities and the frequency of visits may all have to be fine-tuned while introductions are under way. Keeping in step with the child may require a speeding up or a slowing down. Sometimes children are very cautious – they do not demur or complain during introductions but they can drag their feet and seem quite willing for meetings and visits to go on forever.

> *Rachel was nine years old and her prospective adopters were delighted with how smoothly introductions were going according to plan. But when the plan came to an end, Rachel calmly announced that she didn't want to move, and then added 'not yet'. A hastily recalled review meeting scheduled a two-week extension to the initial plan. After one week Rachel phoned the adopters and said, 'Can I come now?' And she did.*

Social workers are faced with a greater dilemma if children or adopters want to cut introductions short. Clearly, everyone has to make sure that it is safe to go ahead and that the placement will not be put at unnecessary risk. The reason for haste and whether or nor all preparatory work has been completed will influence the decision. If prospective permanent carers are ready to take over and the child is ready to move, a flexible approach is required. After one speedy placement, a social worker was rebuked by the head of her department: 'Children are not placed like that,' he said. But sometimes they are.

Danger signals

Many disruption meetings reveal that carers or social workers refrained from making comments during introductions because they didn't want to be the ones to "rock the boat". Sometimes foster carers have said that they were not listened to; sometimes adopters have said that they couldn't face failure, or that one of them had been unable to admit their true feelings to the other. Sometimes the danger signals are evident after the first meeting, but when everyone has invested so much, it is hard to call a halt. And there is always the hope that the situation will improve.

It is not possible to make a list of every danger signal, because each child, their foster carers and their new family will present a mixture with infinite variations. However, some very general indications of risk should be considered with caution.

- Lack of co-operation between the current and prospective families: if mistrust seems to be unfounded, can there be a form of mediation? If they are well founded, how will they be followed up?
- The prospective carers are always late, want to change every item in the plan, and do not willingly report back. Do they want to withdraw?
- The child is having tantrums, nightmares and is distressed at school. Is more preparation needed? Should there be a pause in introductions for therapeutic input?
- The foster carer confides serious reservations to their supervising social worker. Do they have good reason? If not, how can they be reassured?
- One prospective carer is clearly keener than the other to proceed. Was this picked up during assessment? Can the couple talk about it together and with their worker?
- The child is attaching to one parent but forcefully rejecting the other. Can the couple accept and deal with this situation?
- There is serious illness or death in the adoptive, foster or birth family. Should introductions be postponed?
- Children have to believe that, if introductions do not lead to placement, it is not their fault, and it is up to the adults to get it right next time.
- Unless there are safety considerations, prospective permanent carers should understand that, if they cannot become parents to one child, it does not mean that they cannot be the right parents for another.
- If introductions fail, a disruption meeting to identify causes and to make plans for moving on should be set up within six weeks.

To placement

Most children are ready to move between 7-14 days after the

beginning of introductions, if all the preparatory work has been done. But this is a general rule, and it might be more accurate to say that introductions are as long as the proverbial piece of string. Each plan must be tailored to meet the needs of each child and will also depend on the circumstances and capacities of present and future carers. Older children, like Rachel above, may take longer, with meetings at greater intervals, before they are ready to commit, whilst very young children may move quickly after brief, very intensive introductions. The best we can do is to make a plan that fits the purpose, hope that it works and amend it if it doesn't.

Finally, there is the placement day. The supervising social worker should be at hand to support the foster family and the child's social worker should be present for the leave-taking. It is always better for the new family to collect the child than for the child to be "delivered". The minimum of packing should be left until the last moment if the child's belongings have been transferred in stages. Children should leave their foster carers knowing exactly when and where they will see them again.

Marking the child's departure from the foster home and having leaving parties can be difficult for foster carers, who may want to lay on a big event to give everyone who knows the child a chance for a "proper goodbye". Some foster carers see this as a way to show the child how much they care about them, and events like this undoubtedly have a function in helping the foster carers to let the child go. If a party takes place just before the child moves, it can result in children being over-stimulated and over-tired on the day, so it is always better to suggest that any such party is held before the intensive introductions start. The last day/evening spent at the foster home should involve low key/quiet activities, such as a favourite meal chosen by the child and shared with just the foster family.

Good practice points

- Monitor every stage of the introductions by communicating with the child, the foster carers and the adopters/permanent carers before and after meetings and visits.
- Stick to the plan but be flexible if changes are requested and can be agreed with all the people concerned.

- Watch the child and go at the child's place.
- Give everyone the opportunity to voice concerns.
- Celebrate the placement.

> *The whole foster family turned out – and a couple of the social workers came to see us off. They made an occasion out of it – very quiet, but special. Gina remembers it and calls it her adoption day, although she wasn't legally adopted for well over a year.*
>
> (Adopter of Gina, when she was six)

TIP 10

Follow up with post-placement support

Post-placement support must be part of every placement package and agreed well before introductions begin. The end of introductions is also the beginning of the life-long journey together for the new family. The ending and the beginning have to merge to maintain continuity for the child. Placement should never be an abrupt change, but more of a gentle transition, and a natural consequence of introductions.

In the UK today, the average age of a child coming out of the care system and moving to an adoptive placement is four years, but children up to the age of 12, and occasionally even older, are being placed successfully. Clearly these children and their new families will need assistance to follow the transition, so that the child can become a full member of the new family and so that the adults can parent a child who has probably endured a very unsettled early start in life, with all the attendant difficulties.

Post-adoption support is statutory and framed by legislation, but good practice demands that the same kind of support package (in England and Wales and Scotland) should be provided for all permanent foster families. Assessing the support needs of children and their new families should be based on a careful analysis of the information collected about the child's developmental needs, the parenting capacity of the carers and relevant family and environmental factors. When an assessment of the support needs has been completed, it has to be agreed whether and how specific resources can be made available to meet them.

We also have to consider whether existing services in the community can serve to support the family. For example, can a child's needs be met by universal provision (e.g. the NHS) or might specific difficulties mean that the placing authority has to buy in special services?

A framework for post-placement support

After introductions, in the early stages of placement, it is vital that adopters/permanent carers know both whom to contact for support and how to access help available to them. Whatever the relevant legislation, statutory requirements or departmental policy, the initial support plan should cover:

- **Counselling for all parties.** Some children want to have someone outside their own family circles to talk to and others do not. Work on life story books may require continuing help from a social worker, and the new family or the birth family may need help to deal with a variety of issues that can arise. Immediately after placement, and until legal adoption, social work support has to satisfy the regulations, which can only deal with the quantity and not the quality.
- **Health issues.** Many children who have had to be permanently separated from their birth family have physical or emotional problems. It is good practice for families, with the help of the agency medical adviser, to identify the health services their child will need, so that records can be transferred to the new authority before placement. However, transfers do not always work smoothly and needs can change. Further help, advice or guidance may be required at a later stage.

- **Educational needs.** It is also not uncommon for the children we place in permanent families to have special educational needs. Again, the appropriate provision should be agreed before introductions begin; placements have broken down because the records and statements of educational needs have not been sent, or a place in a school was not agreed before the child moved. If private education is deemed necessary, then the financial arrangements must be confirmed before placement. The education system can be difficult to negotiate and families may value the support of experts.

- **Behavioural and developmental issues.** The need for therapeutic services now, which should be put in place immediately, and the possibility of a need for them in the future, must be considered. There is a confusing array of therapy on offer and not all of it available at the point of need. A delay of six months, or even three, can break a placement if the child becomes increasingly distressed or destructive; the wrong therapy, that does not acknowledge the adoption dimension, can do more harm than good. Families often need guidance as well as financial support for private treatments.

> *We had to say whether we thought Lucy needed play therapy or counselling or family therapy – how should we know?*
>
> *(Adopters soon after placement)*

- **Family and social relationships.** It is important that the quality of the child's attachments as well as an assessment of their attachment style are recorded so that the parents, with their support worker, can refer back as and when questions about attachment arise.

> *If only we'd been told how she didn't really let anyone come close. We thought it was just us. The*

> *social worker was new and she had to look it up somewhere. Now we understand, but it's almost too late.*
>
> *(Adopter on the brink of giving up on an adoption after five months)*

- **Continuity and contact arrangements.** Children who have sustained many losses in their lives should not have to lose more people when they move to a permanent home. Most foster carers have an essential part to play in helping a child to maintain continuity during the transition to permanence. The more attached to them a child is, the more urgent it will be for them to remain in the picture. Previous foster carers can demonstrate that the child doesn't have to break established relationships in order to make new ones by providing active links between the past, the present and the future. Far from preventing children from settling, continuing direct contact with previous carers can enable the child to settle more comfortably. Contact with siblings should enable sisters and brothers to continue to share important aspects of their lives. Contact arrangements may need to be supervised, managed or simply supported. The practice of "goodbye visits" with birth parents has to be questioned if we accept that even permanently placed children will always be the children of two families.

> *I believe there is no such thing as "termination" in the relationship between children and their birth families. Even if their parents die, it's not "over". By creating a ritual based on a pretence that the relationship has ended, the child's internal reality is at odds with the external one.*
>
> *(Pavao, 1998, p 97)*

- **Financial matters.** Some families can fight for everything they need but others do not necessarily have a talent for claiming what is their due, and would prefer to have a support worker fight for them. Agreement regarding allowances, grants and financial support for services should leave permanent carers in no doubt about where the money will come from and how it is to be paid. Particularly when a sibling group is placed, radical and immediate means of support for the family must be considered. Transport, housing, equipment for leisure activities and holidays can prove to be major obstacles for an otherwise suitable family. Someone paid to come in and assist with basic household chores to maintain a sense of physical order in the home can free up families to deal with the task of building healthy relationships when introductions lead to placing several children at once. In no case should the introductions and the move be clouded by anxiety about money matters.

- **Special needs.** Children may have special needs because they have an impairment or serous developmental delay and are unable to function in a particular area. Help with aids, adaptations, an incontinence laundry service or complicated transport arrangements may be as important for families as skilled counselling. As one single adopter said, 'I don't pay much attention to the social workers coming in and out, as long as the nappy service is working' (Argent, 2006, p 67).

- **Regular reviews.** It is self-evident that the best-laid plans need to be reviewed at agreed intervals. Needs change, children and their families grow older and social workers leave. Scarce resources may become scarcer while new developments may offer new choices. Support can only be as good as it feels. And if it feels good enough at one stage, it may not feel as good at another.

What seems imperative is that support plans are imaginative, workable and not formulaic. O'Neill writes that 'adoptive parents see good support as being based on partnership, reciprocity, acknowledgement and empathy, open communication, feeling listened to and believed, commitment, responsiveness and reliability' (2003, p 7). These are clearly good foundations upon which to build a working relationship in which the new placement can be supported to be successful.

Good practice points

- Draw up a plan for continuing support based on the needs of the child, the adopters/permanent carers and birth family members.
- Spell out the type of difficulties that it is thought are likely to arise and identify tangible, practical ways of addressing them.
- Think into the future – how might contact with birth family members, for example, be managed, not just immediately but in years to come?
- Be imaginative! Creative packages of support need not always be hugely expensive but can mean the difference between new families feeling overwhelmed and exhausted or feeling confident and supported. Help with practicalities can make all the difference.
- Ensure that adopters have access to other adopters who have "been there and done that", either through an adopters' support group or a "buddy" system. It can be very heartening for new parents to hear about others' experiences and to learn from them how they have survived and prospered.

There is little doubt that placing children with new families is a complex task and that each introduction will confront a unique child with a unique family in a set of unique circumstances. Introductions are an integral part of a long journey for both the child and the new family; how introductions are prepared for, planned and managed will influence the ultimate destination.

Endpiece

In the end, nothing can prepare you for the reality of living with the child. We did have the loveliest introduction and we were grateful for that. It went just like planned and there were no hiccups. We didn't hesitate for one moment. And Ruby couldn't wait to move in. Even the foster mum was happy, though we knew how much she was going to miss her. All the social workers were for it. And we've never regretted our decision. But till a child is living with you, no one can really know what it will be like. The best introduction plan in the world can only help you to take the next step – to the brink. And the step after that is something else!

(Adoptive father of teenager adopted when she was five)

Bibliography

Argent H (2006) *Ten Top Tips on Placing Children*, London: BAAF

Argent H (2008) *Ten Top Tips on Placing Siblings*, London: BAAF

Argent H and Coleman J (2006) *Dealing with Disruption*, London: BAAF

Byrne S (2000) *Linking and Introductions*, London: BAAF

Cairns K (2002) A*ttachment, Trauma and Resilience*, London: BAAF

Cairns K and Fursland E (2008) *Transitions and Endings*, London: BAAF

Carr K (2007) *Adoption Undone*, London: BAAF

Department for Education and Skills (2008) *Practice Guidance in Assessing the Support Needs of Adoptive Families*, London: DfES

Fahlberg V (1994) *A Child's Journey through Placement*, London: BAAF

Gurstenzang S and Freundlich M (2006) *Answering the Call: Finding a fit that will last a lifetime*, available on www.adoptuskids.org

Harnott C and Humphreys H (2004) *Permanence Planning: Notes for practitioners*, London: Social Care Institute for Excellence, ww.scie.org.uk/publications

Harris P (ed) (2006) *In Search of Belonging: Reflections by transracially adopted people*, London: BAAF

Harris P (ed) (2008) *The Colours in Me*, London: BAAF

Herman J (2001) *Trauma and Recovery: From domestic abuse to political terror*, London: Rivers Oram Publishers

James M (2006) *An Adoption Diary*, London: BAAF

Nicholls EA (2005) *The New Life Work Model*, Lyme Regis: Russell House Publishing

Oates J (ed) (2007) *Early Childhood in Focus: Attachment relationships*, London: Open University Press, available at www.bernardvanleer.org

O'Neill C (2003) 'The simplicity and complexity of support', in Argent H (ed) *Models of Adoption Support*, London: BAAF

Pavao JM (1998) *The Family of Adoption*, Boston: Beacon Press

Romaine M with Turley T and Tuckey N (2007) *Preparing Children for Permanence*, London: BAAF

Ryan T and Walker R (2007) *Life Story Work* (2nd edition), London: BAAF

Schofield G and Beek,M (2006) *Attachment Handbook for Foster Care and Adoption*, London: BAAF

Thomas C and Beckford V (1999) *Adopted Children Speaking*, London: BAAF

Ward M (1997) 'Family paradigms and older child adoption: a proposal for matching parents' strengths to children's needs', *The Family Relations Journal*, 46:3

Wise J (2007) *Flying Solo: A single parent's adoption story*, London: BAAF

For children

Betts B and Ahmed A (2003) *My Life Story, who and where?* CD-ROM. Seven inter-active sections with music sound and colour animation.

Camis J (2001) *My Life and Me*, London: BAAF. A life story book that can be adapted for any child. Guidelines for creative use are included.

Foxon J (2001) *Nutmeg Gets Adopted*, London: BAAF

Kahn H (2002 and 2003) *Tia's Wishes and Tyler's Wishes*, London: BAAF

Shah S (2003) *Adoption: What it is and what it means*, London: BAAF

Shah S (2003) *Fostering: What it is and what it means,* London: BAAF

Shah S and Argent H (2006) *Life Story Work: What it is and what it means*, London: BAAF

Useful organisatons

British Association for Adoption and Fostering (BAAF)
Head Office
Saffron House
6–10 Kirby Street
London EC1N 8TS
Tel: 020 7421 2600
www.baaf.org.uk

BAAF Cymru
7 Cleeve House
Lambourne Crescent
Cardiff CF14 5GP
Tel: 029 2076 1155

BAAF Scotland
40 Shandwick Place
Edinburgh EH2 4RT
Tel: 0131 220 4749

BAAF Northern Ireland
Botanic House
1–5 Botanic Avenue
Belfast BT7 1JG
Tel: 028 9031 5494

Adoption UK
46 The Green
South Bar Street
Banbury OX16 9AB
Tel: 01295 752240
www.adoptionuk.org

Family Rights Group
Second Floor
The Print House
18 Ashwin Street
London E8 3DL
Tel: 020 7923 2628
www.frg.org.uk

Fostering Network
87 Blackfriars Road
London SE1 8HA
Tel: 020 7620 6400
www.fostering.net

Fostering Network Scotland
Ingram House, 2nd Floor
227 Ingram Street
Glasgow G1 1DA
Tel: 0141 204 1400
www.fostering.net/scotland

Appendix

Sample agenda for introductions planning meeting

NB. Preferably before this meeting:

i) All attending should be given an extract to read from Vera Fahlberg's 'Moving a child to adoption'. This section of text is available within *A Child's Journey through Placement*, BAAF, 2004, p198. The extract given should be either:

   a) 'Helping a pre-verbal child move into adoption', or

   b) 'Helping a verbal child move into adoption', as appropriate

ii) For interagency placements:

   a) Hold interagency meeting for completion of BAAF Form H1

   b) Form H2 can be partially completed prior to the introductions planning meeting, to save time, and largely overlaps with the content of this guidance note

1) Give out to everyone:

   i) Checklist for introduction of child to adoptive family

   ii) Timetable sheets

2) Any outstanding matters arising from previous Permanency Planning Meeting? – e.g. life history work/book; provision of background information; health reports on child?

3) Statutory notifications

   Family placement team (FPT) administrator to send these out to:

   i) Prospective adopters' local authority SSD

    ii)   Health authority

    iii)   New GP

    iv)   Family finder or social worker (SW) to inform health visitor (adopters to find out who this is) of date on which placement with adopters has been confirmed, requesting health visitor visit asap after this

    v)   FPT administrator to send statutory notice of panel's decision re: matching child with prospective adopters to:

           i)   birth parents

           ii) adopters

    vi)   Adopters to respond to above letter in writing

    vii) Interagency forms to be completed/signed/copied as appropriate

4) Equipment/introduction costs and payments

Clarify agreed costs, i.e.

–   Payment towards equipment

–   Transport costs during introductions

–   Fostering allowance/adoption allowance: clarify how much and when to start/end; bank details to be completed by prospective adopters and passed to FPT administrator

–   What items will go with child? (e.g. clothes/bedding/toys/ bottles/dummies/special items such as hospital cot tags, first clothes, hair snippet, etc.)

NB. Cot mattresses should not be used for different foster children (DoH guidance), so consider this going with child to new placement.

5) Contact

–   One-off meeting with birth parent(s) or others? When? Where? Who will facilitate?

–   Letterbox contact – with whom? Who will make arrangements?

- Initial/ongoing contact between adopters and foster carers post-placement?
- Direct contact with anyone?
- Is anyone else important in child's life?

6) Support

Clarify respective roles re: placement supervision/support

i) Agency support:

- for child (SW); who in SW's absence? (e.g. line manager)
- emergency duty team telephone number
- for adopters (link worker); who in link worker's absence? (e.g. line manager)
- for foster carers (link worker); who in absence? (e.g. adopter's link worker/line manager)

ii) Informal support; from foster carers to adopters – what are the expectations?

7) Reviews

i) Of introductions: to be built into introduction programme

ii) Statutory reviews: to be held after one month; three months; then six-monthly (minimum)

iii) Where to be held?

iv) Who to arrange?

8) Introductions

- General issues, e.g. applicants' work commitments: does anybody have to work a period of notice? Availability of both applicants in daytime/evenings; any period when unavailable?
- State general time-frame envisaged for introductions
- Stress need for this to go at child's pace
- Review of introductions meeting will confirm anticipated date

  - For an older child, where introductions are likely to be over a more lengthy period of time, it is probably appropriate to plan a detailed introduction programme only as far as the review. It is also less appropriate to use the "timetable" sheets

9) Introductions programme

  - Ensure a social worker from the agency is present when adopters first meet with child

  - Draw up in detail

  - Decide who is responsible for drawing up/circulating a "master copy" (usually family finder)

10) Confirm actions

11) Confirm who will type up/circulate minutes to all asap.

(Reproduced with kind permission from Hillingdon Social Services)

(Taken from Byrne, 2000, pp. 30–31)